YOU CHOOSE BOOKS™

The VOTING RIGHTS ACT OF 1965

An Interactive History Adventure

by Michael Burgan

Consultant:
Kenneth Goings
Professor of African-American and African Studies
The Ohio State University

CAPSTONE PRESS
a capstone imprint

You Choose Books are published by Capstone Press,
1710 Roe Crest Drive, North Mankato, Minnesota 56003
www.capstonepub.com

Library of Congress Cataloging-in-Publication Data
Burgan, Michael.
The Voting Rights Act of 1965 : an interactive history adventure / by Michael
Burgan.
pages cm. — (You choose books. You choose: history)
Summary: "In You Choose format, explores the history of the Voting Rights Act
of 1965, including the struggles minorities had in achieving the right to vote,
enforcement of the law, and the Civil Rights movement of the 1960s and 1970s"—
Provided by publisher.
Includes bibliographical references and index.
ISBN 978-1-4914-1803-1 (library binding)
ISBN 978-1-4914-1805-5 (paperback)
ISBN 978-1-4914-1807-9 (eBook PDF)
1. Suffrage—United States—History—20th century—Juvenile literature.
2. Voting—United States—History—20th century—Juvenile literature.
3. Minorities—Suffrage—United States—History—20th century—Juvenile
literature. 4. United States—Politics and government—1963–1969—Juvenile
literature. 5. United States. Voting Rights Act of 1965—Juvenile literature.
I. Title.
JK1846.B87 2015
324.6'20973—dc23   2014032792

Editorial Credits
Kristen Mohn, editor; Bobbie Nuytten, designer; Tracy Cummins, media researcher;
Charmaine Whitman, production specialist

Photo Credits
Alamy: Everett Collection Historical, 81; AP Photo: 68, BH, 41, Bill Hudson,
Cover, Houston Chronicle/ OTHELL O. OWENSBY JR., 92, Perry Aycock,
72; Capstone Press: 10; Corbis: Bettmann, 46, 76, 87, Flip Schulke, 12, 32, 58,
102; Getty Images: Bloomberg/Scott Eells, 105, Don Cravens/The LIFE Images
Collection, 53, Express, 19, MPI, 36, Photo Researchers, 6; The Granger Collection,
26; LBJ Library: Yoichi Okamoto, 64.

Printed in Canada.
092014   008478FRS15

TABLE OF CONTENTS

ABOUT YOUR ADVENTURE

YOU live in a time when minorities are fighting for their rights, including the right to vote. Several states refuse to change laws that restrict voters. What will you do in this struggle for equal rights?

In this book you'll explore how the choices people made meant the difference between life and death. The events you'll experience happened to real people.

Chapter One sets the scene. Then you choose which path to read. Follow the directions at the bottom of each page. The choices you make will change your outcome. After you finish one path, go back and read the others for new perspectives and more adventures.

YOU CHOOSE the path
you take through history.

The Voting Rights Act of 1965 helped overcome voting restrictions many blacks had faced.

THE STRUGGLE TO VOTE

You are living during the 1960s, a time of great change in the United States. Overseas, the country is fighting a war in Vietnam. Feelings against the war lead to massive public protests. Many people are also demanding civil rights for African-Americans. Slavery ended almost 100 years ago, but many blacks still don't receive the same legal treatment as whites.

One of the most important rights is voting. Voters choose who will lead the government. In some states voters can pass laws. But soon after slavery ended, many former slave states tried to strip black male citizens of their new voting rights, even though those rights were guaranteed in the Constitution.

7

Turn the page.

In the late 1800s and early 1900s, voter registration was difficult for southern blacks to complete. They often had to take literacy tests to prove they could read. Many blacks received little or no education, so they struggled to pass the tests.

Other states made people pay a poll tax before they voted. The taxes kept poor people of all backgrounds from voting. But in the South, the greatest effect was on blacks. The efforts to limit voting also affected some Mexican Americans. At times whites also used the threat of violence to keep blacks and others from voting.

After World War II more blacks became involved in the civil rights movement. Some white Americans joined this effort to achieve equality. The movement fought segregation, which separated whites and blacks in many public buildings or forced blacks to ride in the back of buses. Now, in the 1960s, the civil rights movement is also working to register black voters in southern states.

Many white political leaders in the South are resisting the efforts to register black voters. In some counties blacks outnumber whites. White officials there could lose their power if more blacks vote. And racism is still strong across America. Many whites do not accept African-Americans as their equal.

Turn the page.

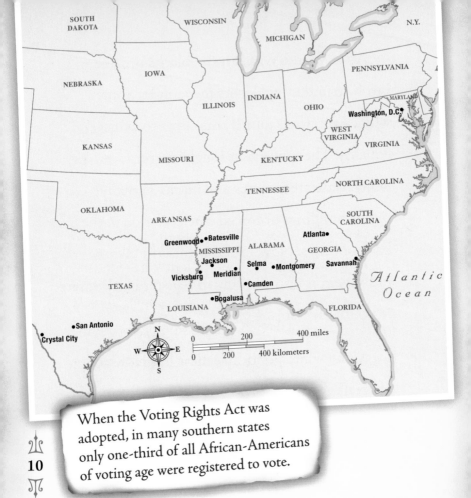

When the Voting Rights Act was adopted, in many southern states only one-third of all African-Americans of voting age were registered to vote.

Several civil rights groups have been calling on the federal government to pass laws to protect everyone's right to vote.

Early in 1964 the country takes an important step when it passes the 24th Amendment to the Constitution. It outlaws poll taxes in federal elections. But states can still collect taxes for state elections. And they can still require literacy tests.

The effort to guarantee everyone's civil rights is growing. But the calls for equality have led to violence in the South. In 1961 a white mob in Alabama attacked civil rights protesters who wanted to end segregation on buses. Now people who call for equal voting rights face violence as well. But you believe all Americans deserve civil rights, and you want to help.

➤ To be a black female volunteer during the 1964 Freedom Summer, turn to page **13**.

➤ To be a white civil rights marcher in Selma, Alabama, in 1965, turn to page **47**.

➤ To be a Mexican-American teen working for Hispanic voting rights around 1970, turn to page **77**.

African-American men placed their ballots at a voting poll in Alabama in 1966.

CHAPTER 2

WORKING THE SUMMER OF FREEDOM

It's April 1964 and you're a young black woman about to graduate from college in your home state of Delaware. Your parents want you to start looking for a job, but you have other plans.

You know civil rights workers in Mississippi are working to help blacks vote. Less than 7 percent of blacks there are registered. Many workers have been arrested for trying to help blacks register. But many people, white and black, want to help blacks vote. So do you.

13

A group called the Student Nonviolent Coordinating Committee (SNCC) is part of that effort in Mississippi. It's seeking college students like you to spend the summer working there.

Turn the page.

In school you're involved with civil rights groups. You've traveled to Maryland and Washington, D.C., to take part in protests. Now you want to join SNCC's Mississippi Summer Project, called the Freedom Summer.

But your father isn't happy about your plan. "It's too dangerous," he says. "You know some black SNCC workers were shot at by whites."

But your mother supports the idea of helping other blacks use their right to vote. She says solemnly, "If you want to help, you should go."

You apply and are accepted by the SNCC. You attend training at a college in Ohio and think about the type of work you'd like. Some of the students will register voters. Others will teach black children at "Freedom Schools."

→ To register voters, go to page **15**.

→ To teach at a Freedom School, turn to page **34**.

In Ohio you meet other volunteers. About 1,000 students have come. You see that white students outnumber black students. You wonder how much they know about the lives of black Americans. But as you get to know some of them, you see that most truly want to help Mississippi blacks.

One of your new white friends is Chris Hilton from Massachusetts. He says that he was impressed by the words of President John F. Kennedy, who was shot and killed last November. President Kennedy inspired many people when he said, "Ask not what your country can do for you; ask what you can do for your country." Chris says helping to end discrimination is one thing he can do.

Turn the page.

Bob Moses, the SNCC worker in charge, teaches you about the conditions in Mississippi. One black man stands and lifts up his shirt, pointing to a scar. "That's where I got shot by a white man who hates the idea of blacks voting." Chris looks as upset as you are.

You also learn about the Ku Klux Klan (KKK). Dressed in white robes and hoods, this violent group often leads the attacks on SNCC volunteers and blacks who try to register.

You can't count on the Mississippi police to protect you. They dislike SNCC's mission. You are horrified to learn that some police even belong to the Klan. You're told that the federal government has no police force that can protect you either.

Despite the violence the volunteers face, SNCC follows the teachings of the Reverend Martin Luther King Jr., a civil rights leader. King urges the use of nonviolent protest. You're taught not to fight back if you're attacked. Instead, you should curl up on the ground to protect yourself. You understand now why your father didn't want you to come.

After the last day of training, most of the volunteers board buses for Mississippi. Some black students you met ask you to ride with them. It's good to spend time with others who understand the problems blacks face. But Chris is heading for another bus, and you would like to talk more with him.

➻To ride with the black volunteers, turn to page **18**.

➻To ride with Chris, turn to page **21**.

Through the night, the bus rolls through Kentucky and Tennessee. Almost everyone is talking and singing. But as the bus reaches the Mississippi state line, everyone goes quiet. Outside the bus are state highway patrol cars. You remember that the police are not there to help you. You realize you face great danger in the weeks ahead.

Around dawn the bus lets you and some other volunteers off by the side of a road. Someone from SNCC is supposed to meet you, but there's no one in sight.

One member of your group, Joseph, has been in Mississippi before with SNCC. He takes charge. "We'll try to stop a car with a black driver and see if he'll take us into town."

A car soon comes and Joseph waves. The driver stops, but then a highway patrol car comes by. The officer tells the driver to move along, and he does. Soon another car approaches. It's filled with loud, young white men. They holler as they drive by. "You're going to end up in the river!" one shouts and throws a glass bottle at your group.

Students from around the world volunteered at the SNCC headquarters in Atlanta, Georgia.

Turn the page.

"We should just kill them right now!" you hear another say as the car speeds away. You feel your knees go rubbery. You can't believe some whites actually feel this way.

Joseph finally gets a black driver to stop. But on the drive you decide you can't spend the summer in Mississippi. You're too scared. You'll go back to Delaware and do the civil rights protests you did before. You want to help others vote, but you're not willing to risk your life.

THE END

To follow another path, turn to page 11.
To read the conclusion, turn to page 103.

"Wait up!" you call out to Chris.

You ride through the night. You see Chris smiling at you a lot. You like him, and you think he likes you too. But he's white and you're black. You know a relationship could never work.

In Batesville, Mississippi, a black farmer named Jim Watson has arranged to take a group of you to his house for dinner. Several of you pile into his van. On the drive, Chris points out the window. "I've never seen anything like this before," he says.

Neither have you. Fields of cotton stretch out all around. Tiny wooden shacks sit along the dirt road. You can't believe that people live in them. Your training didn't prepare you for the harsh poverty in Mississippi.

Turn the page.

At Mr. Watson's house, the local families have prepared a meal for you. They appreciate that you're trying to help them. You feel touched that they are willing to share their food with you.

Chris sits next to you at the meal. He asks you about Delaware and your family. Finally he says, "I know we're not supposed to do this. But when we have some free time, would you like to go on a date?"

You're shocked. Interracial dating is risky, and many blacks and whites disapprove. Also, Bill Johnson, the coordinator for your group, has a rule against volunteers dating one another.

But you like Chris. How much could one date hurt?

→ To say yes, go to page 23.

→ To say no, turn to page 30.

"All right," you say, surprising yourself with your boldness.

That night you stay with the women volunteers at the Watsons. In the dark you see Mr. Watson with a shotgun. "White folks around know you're in town," he says. "I'm going to make sure none of them try to cause any trouble." You're reminded again how dangerous the Freedom Summer will be.

The next morning you're excited to begin visiting some of the people nearby and explaining why they should register to vote. But SNCC has decided that no one will be going out that day for safety precautions. Chris asks if you want to take a walk, and you say yes.

Turn the page.

Going down the road, Chris takes your hand. You wonder if he should do that. People might see you. But you don't let go. You walk and talk all afternoon.

That night Bill calls over you and Chris. "Someone saw you two holding hands today," he says. You feel your heart start to pound. "I'm sorry, but I told you before, volunteers are not allowed to date. It's also dangerous in this area."

Chris looks at you. "I'm willing to leave to be with you," he says.

You like him a lot, but you really care about the work you came to do. And you're not sure you're willing to face the harassment you'll both get for interracial dating.

➤ To go with Chris, go to page 25.

➤ To stay, turn to page 26.

"It's not fair that we can't go together," you tell Bill.

"Fair or not, it's my rule," Bill says.

"Come on," Chris says, taking your hand. You see Bill shaking his head as you both walk away. "We can go up north, to Massachusetts," Chris says.

"If I'm not staying here, I should go home and volunteer there," you say.

"Then I'll go with you to Delaware," he says. "We can work together."

You're glad Chris is serious about helping blacks, even if you won't be doing it in Mississippi. You and Chris don't share the same skin color, but you do share the same values. That's what's important. You just wish the rest of the world saw it that way.

THE END

To follow another path, turn to page 11.
To read the conclusion, turn to page 103.

"Dating can wait," you say to Chris. "The voter registration is more important than us." You tell Bill, "I'm staying."

Chris nods, respecting your decision. "You're right," he says. "Everyone in Mississippi deserves the right to vote, and we need to do our part."

"Glad to hear it," Bill says. "But you can't both stay here."

Civil rights workers helped an African-American couple register to vote in Mississippi in 1964.

Bill arranges for you to go to the Greenwood SNCC office. You miss Chris, but you're soon distracted by the hard work of looking for voters. The summer heat in Mississippi is worse than anything you've ever felt before. Mosquitoes buzz around you constantly. When you finish the day's work, you're careful to go inside before dark. You learned during training that nighttime is when the Klan attacks blacks.

As you start to canvass small towns, you see how the poor blacks of Mississippi live. You go into their simple homes, which often don't have running water. Children pour buckets of cold water over themselves to wash. Some don't have clothes to wear. Most have little to eat.

Turn the page.

Many of the people you meet are sharecroppers. They rent their farmland and give part of what they grow to the whites who own the land. The sharecroppers could be evicted if the white owners find out they want to register to vote. Often, when you ask people to register, they just shake their heads and turn away. For them, getting the right to vote is not worth risking their livelihood. They have to feed their families.

The white people you see in Greenwood are not happy that you and other volunteers are in town. One hot day as you're returning to the office, you notice an older white man following you.

"We don't want your kind around here," he says angrily.

You begin to walk faster. "This town is for white people," he calls out louder. Then he begins to swear—he uses words you've never heard any man say to a woman, white or black. Finally you reach the office and hurry inside.

Miriam, the coordinator, sees the look of terror on your face. "What happened?" she asks.

You tell her and then add, "Besides being scared, I'm frustrated. No one will register. Maybe I should just go home."

"Well, I could use some help here," Miriam says. "If you could work inside the office, would you be willing to stay?" You hug Miriam with relief, glad you can still help with the Freedom Summer.

THE END

To follow another path, turn to page 11.
To read the conclusion, turn to page 103.

"No, Chris," you say. "We can't risk being sent home."

Chris understands, and you agree to stay friends. After Batesville your group is sent to Greenwood. The men do most of the canvassing for possible voters. SNCC doesn't want to increase the chances of the women facing violence. You work in the SNCC office. Most of the women volunteers do paperwork or teach at the Freedom Schools. But even being in the office does not mean you're safe—someone set fire to it last year.

Some nights you go to meetings held in Greenwood. By July hundreds of local residents go to these meetings to discuss civil rights. Often they chant, "Freedom Now!"

On July 16 you take part in a protest outside the courthouse. You hold a sign calling for blacks to register. All around are police wearing helmets and holding nightsticks. Even though it is a peaceful protest, the police surge into the crowd. You hope the many reporters and photographers in the crowd will show the country what's happening in Mississippi.

One of the police grabs a young white man next to you. "Stop!" you yell. "He hasn't done anything wrong! We have a right to protest."

"Not here in Greenwood," another cop says. "Let's go."

Turn the page.

You're terrified as he grabs your wrist too and starts dragging you to a bus already filled with other protesters. Along the way you see Stokely Carmichael, one of the SNCC leaders. The police jolt him with electricity from a cattle prod, and you fight to hold back tears. You're arrested along with more than 100 others.

Stokely Carmichael, who later changed his name to Kwame Ture, was a leader of the SNCC.

In jail you are crammed into a cell with other black women. When dinner comes, you taste a plate of beans and rice but spit it out. One of the officers has poured extra black pepper into it. You can't believe how badly you're treated, simply for trying to help people.

"We should go on a hunger strike!" one woman yells.

You agree. You want the police to know you still have the will to protest. You won't eat anything as long as you're in jail. It shouldn't be too long. All the volunteers were instructed to bring money to pay for bail in case of arrest. Soon you hope to be back on the streets, fighting for civil rights for all.

THE END

To follow another path, turn to page 11.
To read the conclusion, turn to page 103.

At a Freedom School, you can use some of your teaching experience from college. During training you learn how bad the regular schools are in Mississippi for black children. The state spends much less money to educate them than they spend for white students. And the black students learn nothing about black history in America.

One day Bob Moses, who runs the Mississippi Summer Project, shares some awful news. On June 21 three volunteers went to investigate a church bombing in Longdale, Mississippi. They never returned to the local volunteer office. A small white woman gets up and asks you all to write to the members of Congress from your state. "Demand that the federal government investigate what happened!" she pleads.

Someone near you whispers, "That's Rita Schwerner. Her husband, Mickey, is one of the men who's missing."

The news upsets you. But some are not so worried. Maybe the three got arrested and just can't call for help. You try to believe that.

At the end of the week, an SNCC worker named Charlie Cobb comes over to you. "Would you like to teach in a city, like Vicksburg? Or would you prefer a rural school?" he asks. You're used to living in a city. You might be more comfortable in Vicksburg. But maybe the students in rural areas need your help more.

→ To go to a rural area, turn to page **36**.

→ To go to Vicksburg, turn to page **41**.

Schools, churches, and even stores served as polling places for voters.

"I'll take a rural area," you tell Charlie.

"Good," he says. "We'll send you just outside of Meridian." You gulp. Meridian is where the three missing Summer Project workers were based.

"Will it be safe?" you ask.

Charlie shakes his head. "Nowhere is safe for us in Mississippi this summer." You remind yourself what you signed up for and try to put on a brave face.

On the last day of training, Bob Moses speaks to everyone again. "The missing volunteers are dead," he announces. "There may be more deaths."

Moses keeps talking, but you barely hear the words. You knew volunteering was dangerous. But you hadn't actually thought you could be killed. Some students are crying. But most say they will still go to Mississippi. You slip out of the hall to use the pay phone. You call your mother and tell her what has happened.

"Come home," she pleads. "You can still do your part to help blacks get their rights. Just don't do it in Mississippi!"

→ To go to Mississippi, turn to page **38**.

→ To go home, turn to page **42**.

"Mom," you say, "you told me how important it is to help other blacks. And I still believe that, even with the risks. I'm going to Mississippi." You hear your mother cry, but she tells you she's proud of your courage.

Before you get on the bus for Mississippi, Charlie tells you there's a change in plans. You'll be going to a town called Canton, north of Jackson. "The whites there have already said they don't like the idea of a Freedom School," Charlie says. "So don't expect an easy stay."

"I'm ready," you say, though you're not sure you are.

When you arrive, there's already been trouble. "Someone broke into the library and destroyed all the books," a local volunteer explains. "And some men have been calling black families saying they'll bomb their houses if they send their kids to school."

"We're still going to open that school," you say, determined not to let the local racists stop you.

The black parents, though, are afraid of the bomb threats. On the first day of school, they keep their children home. You and another volunteer go door to door seeking students.

Turn the page.

"We have to teach the children," you say to one mother. "The state doesn't care about them. Your children need to know their rights—and how to read and write."

The mother looks you in the eye. "You gave up a lot to come down here and help us," she says. "You're taking a chance."

You nod. Then the mother continues, "Then I guess I can too." She agrees to send her daughter to the Freedom School. Soon other parents do too. You feel proud of yourself for working so hard to help these kids get the same chance you had to get an education.

40

THE END

To follow another path, turn to page 11.
To read the conclusion, turn to page 103.

The next week you begin teaching in Vicksburg. It's hard work, but you love it. The students are eager to learn about black history. You soon see how badly they were educated before.

As the summer winds down, you think about how you'll miss the children and the friends you've made. You spend a lot of time together at the Freedom House, where you're staying. You also spend time riding together to and from the Freedom House. SNCC requires you all to travel in groups for safety. But one afternoon there's no room for you in the car going back to the house. You can wait for another one to come by, but maybe it would be quicker to walk.

→ *To wait for another car, turn to page 43.*

→ *To start walking, turn to page 44.*

A volunteer from Brooklyn, New York, taught black students in Jackson, Mississippi, in 1964.

You think about the three volunteers killed in Mississippi. You imagine your parents' pain if something happened to you.

"I'll get a bus tomorrow," you tell your mother. "I'm coming home." You're disappointed, but you know you could not be a good teacher if you were always terrified.

THE END

To follow another path, turn to page 11.
To read the conclusion, turn to page 103.

A car approaches, but you soon realize something is wrong. There are four people inside—and they're all wearing white robes and hoods. A Klansman jumps out and pulls you into the car.

One of the men growls at you, "Girl, you're going to be sorry you ever came to Mississippi!" The car stops in an empty lot. The men pull you out. You want to scream, but you say nothing as they whip you with a rubber hose. Tears fill your eyes as pain fills your body. Finally, they leave.

When you find the strength to get up, you begin to walk back to the Freedom House. You fall into the arms of your friends, grateful to be alive.

THE END

To follow another path, turn to page 11.
To read the conclusion, turn to page 103.

You start to walk, sticking as close to the buildings and as far from the street as possible. You constantly turn your head, looking for signs of trouble. You heart pounds with every step.

You're close to the Freedom House when you hear a car coming up behind you. You walk a little faster. The car gets closer and your fear heightens, but then someone calls your name. You look over and see Sara, one of your students, in the car. The woman driving must be her mother. You breathe a sigh of relief and stop to chat.

"Oh, Sara, it's good to see you," you say.

Sara's mother reaches out to shake your hand. "I just want to tell you how much Sara enjoys you and your class," she says. "It's a blessing, what all you Freedom Summer people are doing for us."

She asks if you would like to come to their house for dinner. You tell her you would like that very much. But first you must stop by the Freedom House so no one there will worry about you.

As you talk with Sara and her mother that evening, you feel proud that you've come to Mississippi. You really are making a difference in the lives of the people here.

THE END

To follow another path, turn to page 11.
To read the conclusion, turn to page 103.

The Reverend James
J. Reeb from Boston
worked in support
of the civil rights
movement and the
Voting Rights Act.

CHAPTER 3

THE HEROES OF SUMMER

"Some of my deepest concerns have related to the problems of Negro people in our society. I would like to have a further opportunity to contribute to the changes that will bring them full equality."

You listen to the words of James J. Reeb, the minister of your church. Like you, Reeb is white, but he is committed to helping blacks win the rights they deserve.

It's July 1964 and you live outside of Boston. You've just finished your third year of college. Like Reverend Reeb, your family supports civil rights for all. You're happy when President Lyndon Johnson signs the Civil Rights Act. The law will help end discrimination against blacks.

Turn the page.

Blacks in Massachusetts have always had an easier time voting than those living in southern states. The protests and violence in the South seem distant from your daily life.

That changes in March 1965. Reverend Reeb hears about the violence that took place in Selma, Alabama, as blacks sought their right to vote. The blacks in Selma wanted to march to Montgomery, the Alabama capital. They wanted state leaders to know that blacks deserved their rights.

But before they left Selma, the police attacked them. And Governor George Wallace would not allow the marchers to use a major highway. In Selma white residents cheered as the police swung their nightsticks at the marchers and released tear gas. As many as 100 people were injured.

Reverend Martin Luther King Jr. is a leader of the civil rights movement. He has sent a message to Reverend Reeb and other black and white ministers across the country. He wants them to come to Selma and show their support by marching. The ministers ask people in their churches to come along. You ask your parents if you can go.

"Of course the blacks down south deserve the right to vote," your mother says. "But let the government handle it. You don't need to get involved—it could be dangerous."

"But wanting to help others is a good thing," you say. "That's what you always say."

→ To go to Selma, turn to page **50**.

→ To stay home, turn to page **65**.

"I know it could be dangerous," you say. "But I can't sit back and do nothing."

Your parents finally agree to let you go. Reverend Reeb goes to Selma and gives you the name of someone to contact when you get there. Rob Harrison works for the Southern Christian Leadership Conference (SCLC). It's one of the civil rights groups working in Selma, and Reverend King is one of its leaders. Rob meets you at the bus station, and he doesn't look happy.

"Something terrible happened last night," Rob says. "Reverend Reeb and two other ministers were attacked on the street."

You feel like you could be sick. "What, what happened?" you stutter.

Rob explains how a group of four white men beat up the ministers. The men knew the ministers had come to Selma to support voting rights for blacks. "From what I heard," Rob continues, "one guy swung a 3-foot pipe at Reverend Reeb's head. He's in the hospital."

"Is he badly hurt?"

Rob just lowers his head. Tears fill your eyes. Reverend Reeb is a good man. You pray that he will be all right.

"Are you still willing to stay?" Rob asks you.

You know your parents will be even more worried than before. But you'd like to carry on the work Reverend Reeb came here to do.

→To go home, turn to page **52**.

→To stay in Selma, turn to page **53**.

The next day you head home. "We're so glad you're safe!" your mother says at the airport.

Two days later you read in the newspaper that Reverend Reeb has died. On March 15 President Johnson goes on TV to promote his proposed Voting Rights Act. He says the new voting law "will strike down restrictions to voting in all elections—Federal, State, and local—which have been used to deny Negroes the right to vote."

Over the next few months, you pay close attention as the Voting Rights Act goes through Congress. Finally, on August 6, 1965, Johnson signs the law. Reverend Reeb would have approved. You're sorry he's not here to see this historic moment.

THE END

To follow another path, turn to page 11.
To read the conclusion, turn to page 103.

Marchers protested the attack on Reverend Reeb in front of the Alabama capitol.

"I came to help support civil rights. I'm not going home," you say.

Rob is glad you've decided to stay. "But what we're doing isn't easy," he says. "Come with me. Let me show you what it's like."

Turn the page.

Rob takes you to a street where some people are still waiting to hear if the march will go on. They stand in the rain. Rows of local and state police block the protesters from moving. Behind the police a crowd of white men has gathered. They hurl insults at the people waiting to march. Suddenly you see one of the men throw something toward you.

"Look out!" you yell and push Rob out of the way. A large rock lands near his feet. "Why are they doing that?" you ask.

"They want us to respond with violence," Rob says. "Then the police will have a reason to start beating and arresting us."

"But the police won't arrest the whites who throw the rocks?" you ask.

Rob shakes his head. "Never." Rob also explains that the Alabama state government still does not want a march to take place. The SCLC and other civil rights groups have gone to court to win the right to march. A judge in Montgomery has to decide if the protesters can go from Selma to Montgomery.

Some people are heading to Montgomery to protest in front of the courthouse there. Rob asks if you want to go. But he's also heard some people might drive to the hospital where Reverend Reeb is being treated. It would be good to see him.

➤ To go to Montgomery, turn to page **56**.

➤ To stay in Selma, turn to page **62**.

You board a bus for Montgomery with members of a civil rights group called the Student Nonviolent Coordinating Committee (SNCC). It has been very active in trying to help blacks vote. When you reach Montgomery, you see black and white college students and other young people everywhere.

The large mass marches to the state capitol, where dozens of state police guard the doorway. They refuse to let the protesters get close to the building. Some of the leaders want to talk to Governor George Wallace, but he refuses to see them. Wallace has resisted efforts to end segregation or give blacks more rights.

More police arrive. You see a few officers swinging their nightsticks. You watch in disbelief as one approaches you and raises his stick. You've done nothing wrong! You fall to the ground and curl up, just as the other protesters are doing. You scream when the blow from the stick comes down hard on your arm. The officer moves on, looking for someone else to hit.

An older black woman comes over to help you. She says her name is Jean Pierce and that she works at one of the black colleges. "You need to get off the street," she says. "You might have broken your arm." You want to stay with the protestors, but she might be right about your arm.

→ *To stay at the protest, turn to page* **58**.

→ *To leave the protest, turn to page* **61**.

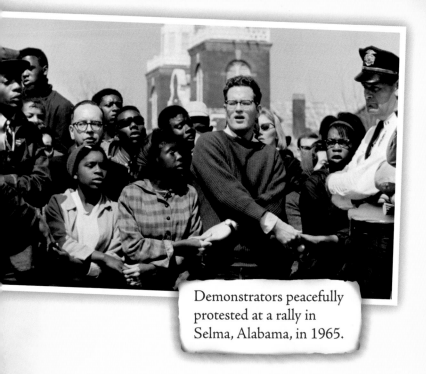

Demonstrators peacefully protested at a rally in Selma, Alabama, in 1965.

"Thank you, but I'll be all right," you tell Jean.

As the day goes on, some students return to their schools. But hundreds remain in the street in front of the capitol. You worry when a group of police on horses approaches the crowd. "They're going to charge!" someone yells. Mounted police called possemen had attacked people in Selma just days before.

One of the possemen shouts, "Leave, all of you! Now!"

"Just sit down," a protestor near you says. You feel your heart racing as you sit. Slowly everyone around you does too. And the possemen don't charge!

"How did you know they wouldn't charge?" you ask the man.

"There are a lot of newspaper reporters around," he says. "The possemen know the reporters will tell everyone what happens here. They'd look bad if they attacked for no reason."

But you feel your skin crawl as the officers shout insults at the blacks around you. The police are supposed to serve and protect everyone. Now you see that here in Alabama, that doesn't apply to blacks.

Turn the page.

The possemen finally back away. The police tell the crowd that people may leave to go the bathroom and will be allowed to return. You head for the restrooms. When you return, a police officer stops you. "But we were told we could leave and come back," you say.

"Go back home where you belong," the officer says. You push past him with your good arm. "What do you think you're doing?" he yells.

"I have a right under the Constitution to assemble with others to express my views," you quote from the First Amendment.

"The only thing you're going to do is spend a night in jail." You're arrested, but you feel proud for speaking out against discrimination.

THE END

To follow another path, turn to page 11.
To read the conclusion, turn to page 103.

Jean leads you to a nearby church. You wait there until you can arrange a ride back to Selma. On the drive, your arm starts to throb with pain. You're not sure you can take another violent protest. You decide to go home.

Your parents are glad to see you the next day, but your mother worries about your arm. "I'm fine," you say. But you're devastated—and angry—when you learn Reverend Reeb died from his injuries.

The next Monday you tell your friends about your experience in Alabama. Some think you were crazy to get involved. Others admire your courage. You're glad that you took a stand for equality for blacks, just as Reverend Reeb did.

THE END

To follow another path, turn to page 11.
To read the conclusion, turn to page 103.

"I'll stay here," you tell Rob. He leads you away from the crowd on the street. "I know that blacks are denied their right to vote," you say, "but can't they go to the courts to get help?"

Rob shakes his head. "Maybe they don't tell you what goes on down here," he says. "Black people have gone to court for their rights. But here in Alabama and Mississippi, lots of judges are as racist as the guy who threw that rock at us. The judges find reasons to toss out the cases."

You understand now why Reverend Reeb always talked about equal justice. Having laws doesn't mean anything if they only help some people and not others.

The next day, Rob comes to you with a sad face. "It's Reverend Reeb," he says.

You know right away what's happened. Reverend Reeb has died. Rob puts his hand on your shoulder. "Do you want to go home?" he asks.

"No. I have stay," you choke out. "For Reverend Reeb. For equal rights."

On March 17 a judge finally rules that the march can go on, but only some marchers can go all the way to Montgomery. Four days later you march with about 3,000 people. Leading the way is Reverend King. Blacks and whites from across the country have come to take part. Soldiers line the route to protect you from anyone seeking to harm you. But many people still shout insults.

Turn the page.

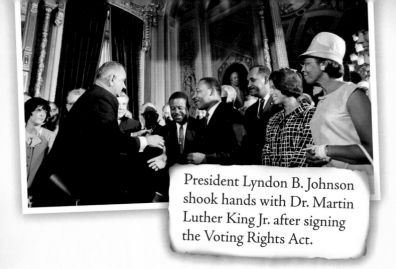

President Lyndon B. Johnson shook hands with Dr. Martin Luther King Jr. after signing the Voting Rights Act.

Like most of the marchers, you'll turn back tonight at the first stop. About 300 others continue all the way to Montgomery. On March 25 you join them to hear King address a crowd of 25,000 people. He talks about blacks' right to vote and ending segregation. He praises President Johnson for supporting the Voting Rights Act.

That summer the Voting Rights Act becomes law. You believe you played a small part in making that happen.

THE END

To follow another path, turn to page 11.
To read the conclusion, turn to page 103.

Your mother is right. Alabama might be too dangerous. Besides, you can't miss too many classes.

A few days later, the newspaper reports some terrible news. Reverend Reeb has been badly beaten in Selma. A group of white men attacked him because he had come to help blacks vote. Later, word comes that Reeb is dead. You decide that when you graduate in May, you will join the civil rights movement.

Turn the page.

One day in April, you see a poster at school. A program called Summer Community Organizing and Political Education (SCOPE) wants volunteers. They will travel across the South to register blacks to vote. SCOPE is a project of the Southern Christian Leadership Conference (SCLC). This civil rights group played a large part in organizing the Selma march, which finally took place after Reverend Reeb's death.

Since the march, Congress has been working on the Voting Rights Act. SCLC leaders believe it will become law by the end of June. The law will make it easier for SCOPE volunteers to help blacks register to vote. You tell your parents you want to volunteer.

Your father agrees. "Blacks in the South have been denied their rights for too long. And who knows if the Voting Rights Act will really help." In June your parents pay for your plane flight to Atlanta, Georgia, where you'll be trained. Before you go, your father hands you $100—a large sum of money. He whispers in your ear, "Be careful."

Hundreds of white college students come to Atlanta for the training. Black volunteers and SCLC workers are there as well. On the first day, you listen to a speech by Reverend Martin Luther King Jr. He describes how SCOPE will help blacks vote and improve their lives.

Turn the page.

African-American protesters and Klansmen both demonstrated on an Atlanta street in 1964.

During the training, you learn that, as in Selma, you could face violence. But SCOPE does not believe in fighting back. You're given a choice of where to work. You think about Alabama, since Reverend Reeb had gone there. But Dick Rivers, a white volunteer from Georgia you've met, is going to stay in the state. He has plenty of friends around, and it could be good to have support.

➤ To stay in Georgia, go to page **69**.

➤ To go to Alabama, turn to page **73**.

You, Dick, and two other SCOPE volunteers join SCLC workers to drive to Chatham County, Georgia. One of the black workers, Sam Wells, explains that the white volunteers should duck whenever they see another car.

"The whites around here don't like to see blacks and whites together," Sam says. "If they see us, they'll get suspicious. They could call the police—or the Ku Klux Klan."

You see that your work in Chatham won't be easy. The Voting Rights Act has not passed yet, as SCLC thought it would. Blacks still face literacy tests. Many blacks want to wait for the new law to take effect before registering to vote.

Turn the page.

Sam explains that for poor people with little education, the literacy tests are almost impossible to pass. He asks you, "Could you explain any passage from your state constitution? One that a voting official picks out for you on the spot?"

"I doubt it," you say.

"And you've been to college," Sam goes on. "But that's what some blacks still have to do before they're allowed to vote."

You also hear about SCOPE offices in other cities being bombed. Some volunteers have been shot at by white racists. But you feel safe until one day in a small town outside Savannah. Dick runs to buy something from a grocery store. While you wait, you see a pickup truck with three white men inside. The truck stops and two of the men get out. They're holding lead pipes.

Before you can say or do anything, the two men sprint toward you, swinging. "We don't want your kind around here!" one says.

"This is what we do to you white northerners so concerned about civil rights," the other snarls before swinging a pipe.

Turn the page.

Demonstrators were injured after mounted police broke up a voting rights march in Montgomery, Alabama, in 1965.

Dick sees you on the street and rushes over. The attackers flee. "Are you all right?"

The beating lasted only a few seconds. But it was long enough to leave your face bloodied and a rib cracked. You've now had a glimpse of the discrimination southern blacks are facing.

THE END

To follow another path, turn to page 11.
To read the conclusion, turn to page 103.

You and several other volunteers drive to Camden, Alabama. The local mayor is not happy that SCOPE has come to town.

"We don't have any civil rights problems around here," he says. But blacks in town tell you a different story. They're glad SCOPE has come to help them get equal rights.

After several days of canvassing, you see what you're up against. You see carloads of young whites driving by, giving dirty looks. You meet some local white college students who are interested in your work. But when the mayor finds out, he tells the students' parents. The parents forbid their children to get involved.

Turn the page.

In July you hear about protest marches going on in Bogalusa, Louisiana. Several volunteers want to take part. "The white leaders there won't enforce the 1964 Civil Rights Act," your friend Deborah says. "And if blacks try to assert themselves, they're beaten."

You agree to go. When you reach Bogalusa, you see hundreds of people marching in the streets. A local judge has ordered police to protect civil rights workers and protesters. But the police ignore it, so mobs of white racists are allowed to beat up protesters.

You join a group of people picketing outside a store that discriminates against blacks. While the police ignore violence against the protesters, they instead begin to arrest the picketers—including you!

That night you call your parents from the crowded Bogalusa jail. You explain about leaving Alabama and coming to Bogalusa. "It's terrible, Dad," you say. "The whites beat up the blacks and no one does a thing to stop it. There was blood everywhere."

"It could have been your blood," your father says quietly. "Will you stop protesting and go back to work with SCOPE?"

You promise to return to SCOPE. After a pause your father says, "I'm very proud of you. It's important for whites to be involved."

As you hang up, you feel a warm glow. Your father thinks you're doing something important—and you think so too.

THE END

To follow another path, turn to page 11.
To read the conclusion, turn to page 103.

In 1971 a Chicano group marched 600 miles across California to protest discrimination against Americans of Mexican descent.

CHAPTER 4

THE RISE OF CHICANO POWER

"It makes me so angry," your mother says.

"What does?" you ask her.

"You know that I don't read and write English so well," she says. "But every time I try to vote, the election workers won't help me read the ballot. They say it's against the state law. Why doesn't the Voting Rights Act apply in Texas too?"

You are a high school student living with your family in southern Texas. Your grandparents came from Mexico, but you, your parents, and most of your relatives are U.S. citizens. Despite that, and the passage of the 1965 Voting Rights Act, Mexican Americans sometimes have trouble voting.

Turn the page.

You read in school about the Voting Rights Act. In some southern states, the laws only apply in counties with large black populations. In many places, Mexican Americans and American Indians still face discrimination when they try to vote.

At one time people in Texas had to pay a tax before they could vote. Wealthy white farmers paid the tax for their Mexican workers. But the farmers forced the workers to vote a certain way. The workers knew they would lose their jobs if they didn't follow orders. The poll taxes are now illegal. But some whites in this part of Texas still resist letting Mexicans vote or play a role in local politics.

"Things are not so good here for us Mexican Americans," your father says. "There's so much prejudice. Maybe we should move up to Yakima, Washington, with my brother Fernando. There's plenty of farm work and the pay is better than in Texas."

Your father says that Fernando wrote recently, inviting your whole family to visit. "Your mother and I need to work," your father says. "But maybe you can go up for the summer and let us know what you think."

You feel proud that your father trusts your judgment, and you like the idea of visiting your cousins and seeing a different part of the country. But Washington is far away. It might be scary to travel that far by yourself.

➤ To go to Washington, turn to page **80**.

➤ To stay in Texas, turn to page **91**.

When you arrive in Yakima, Uncle Fernando greets you warmly. Your cousin Tomas tells you about what he's been doing at his college.

"I joined a group called the United Farm Workers Cooperative (UFWC). We're trying to improve the lives of the Chicanos here in Washington."

Tomas laughs when you ask what a Chicano is. "You're a Chicano, cousin! A Chicano is anyone who traces his roots to Mexico. And like the blacks, it's time we Chicanos demand our rights!"

He tells you about a man named Cesar Chavez. In California he's trying to improve the pay and working conditions for migrant workers. Tomas' group is based on one Chavez founded. One issue the group is working on is voting rights.

"Chavez tried to register Mexicans in California years ago," Tomas says. "We can register here, but they make some Mexicans take literacy tests first. And when we do register, the county won't give Spanish ballots to those who can't read English." You nod and tell him that Texas has similar problems.

Cesar Chavez was the leader of the United Farm Workers group and an advocate for Chicano civil rights.

Turn the page.

"We have to demand our legal rights everywhere," Tomas says. "If we can't vote, how will we ever pass laws that help Chicanos get better education and jobs?"

"It's just not fair," you say.

Tomas invites you to a meeting. You think you might like to hear about Tomas' group. But your father wanted you to learn about farming in Yakima. He might not want you to get involved with politics.

➻ To go with Tomas to a meeting, go to page 83.

➻ To say no, turn to page 90.

Tomas takes you to Toppenish, the city where the UFWC was started. The UFWC is working with a legal group called the American Civil Liberties Union (ACLU). It helps people who've been denied their rights. The group wants to help Mexican Americans use their legal right to vote.

At the meeting a man name Caesario Jimenez explains what happened to him when he tried to register to vote. In Spanish he says, "They told me I could not register because I can't read or write English. I talked to some other workers, and they experienced the same thing. We are all U.S. citizens. This is not right!"

Turn the page.

A lawyer from the ACLU named Charles Ehlert stands. "We have found three other people who are willing to challenge Yakima County in court," he says. "The state can't ask Mexican Americans to come here to work and then deny them their vote."

People in the crowd shout their approval. Ehlert says his group will bring other lawsuits too, to help create better conditions for migrant workers.

After the meeting Tomas says to you, "There's a lot to be done to protect Chicano rights. Maybe you can stay up here this fall and help."

You'd like to help, but you also need to make sure you finish high school so you can graduate next year.

➤ *To stay in Yakima, go to page* **85**.

➤ *To go back to Texas, turn to page* **88**.

The next day you talk to Uncle Fernando about staying in Yakima and going to school there. Your parents trust Tomas and Fernando to take care of you. And they are proud that you want to help Mexican Americans get their rights.

In the fall you start high school in Yakima. Around the same time, the ACLU begins the legal process to challenge the law requiring voters to read and write English. Ehlert says that the 1965 Voting Rights Act was meant to stop that kind of discrimination.

Turn the page.

On weekends you go with Tomas to Seattle. Chicano students there are calling for a boycott of grapes that aren't picked by migrant workers in unions. The unions fight for better pay for the workers, and some grape growers don't like them. They don't want to have to offer the better pay and conditions that the unions require. At one protest a group of young white men begin yelling insults at the Chicanos.

"Go back to Mexico!" one shouts.

"I was born here," Tomas shouts back. "I'm just as American as you!"

The man and his friends walk toward you and Tomas. "You better get out of here," Tomas mutters to you. "There could be trouble."

"No way. I'm staying with you."

The men keep
approaching, but a police
officer nearby steps in.
You don't hear what he
says, but the men turn
away. The officer turns
to Tomas and says, "You
better be careful what
you say. Next time there
might not be a cop
around to help." Tomas
just nods.

Civil rights demonstrators
marched August 7, 1971,
to protest discrimination
against Mexican Americans.

You're glad the officer stopped the men. But it
makes you sad to think Mexican Americans face
such prejudice. It's that kind of racism that makes
it so hard for some of them to vote.

THE END

To follow another path, turn to page 11.
To read the conclusion, turn to page 103.

You need to get back to your family and school. When the summer ends, you board a bus for Texas. But you tell Tomas to write with news about Caesario Jimenez and his lawsuit.

The case finally goes before three federal judges in April 1969. Tomas sends you newspaper articles about it. Jimenez and the others went to register with interpreters who would help them fill out the paperwork. But the election officials said that was not legal.

The judges decide that asking Jimenez and the others if they read and write English was not the same as a literacy test. That meant the election officials had not done anything wrong. The Mexican Americans trying to vote were no better off than they were before.

You are disappointed when you read that Jimenez will not have the right to vote just because he doesn't speak English. But Tomas tells you it's not over yet. The ACLU will bring the case to the U.S. Supreme Court. The Court could reverse the lower court's decision. You hope it does. But you also realize that you and all Mexican Americans will have to keep fighting to protect your right to vote.

THE END

To follow another path, turn to page 11.
To read the conclusion, turn to page 103.

You tell Tomas you're too young to get involved in politics. But you like that he wants Chicanos to have the same rights as everyone else.

"You're not too young to help," Tomas says. "High school students in Los Angeles had a huge protest this year for Chicano rights."

That fall, back in Texas, you tell your parents everything Tomas is doing to help Mexican Americans. You explain about the growing Chicano movement and that you want to get involved. "I want to make sure you can vote without any troubles," you say. "And that I'll never have to face the discrimination other Chicanos have faced."

THE END

To follow another path, turn to page 11.
To read the conclusion, turn to page 103.

You tell your parents you'd prefer to stay home for the summer. Your family hopes that maybe you'll all be able to make the trip next year.

When fall comes, people in town prepare for local elections. You wonder if any Mexican Americans will ever get elected. Even though the town is mostly Hispanic, many of them don't vote. That allows white voters to control the election.

"We should do like they did in Crystal City," your father says. He explains that in 1963, the Mexican Americans there ran candidates for the city council. Then they actively registered Hispanic voters and convinced them to vote. For two years the Mexican Americans controlled the council, until powerful white business owners took control again.

Turn the page.

Huelga Schools in Houston, Texas, were created to educate Hispanic students who were boycotting public schools because of unfair treatment.

But no Hispanics are on the ballot in your town. Once again the whites will control things, even though Mexican Americans outnumber them. Your father is disgusted. "Maybe it's time to leave here after all," he says. "We can move up to Washington, or go to Mexico."

"I don't want to leave," your mother says. "All our friends are here. And the discrimination we face is nothing new."

Your father turns to you. "What about you? Do you want to stay?"

You do hate that you can't speak Spanish in school. And you never learn about Mexican Americans and what they've done for the United States. But your friends and your whole life are here too.

➤ To say you want to leave, turn to page **94**.

➤ To ask to stay, turn to page **95**.

"Maybe we should go," you say, sadly.

After lots of discussion, it is decided. You will go to Mexico. "We have plenty of relatives there who will help us," your father says. "The economy is better than when our parents immigrated here. We will be all right. And I won't have to worry about anyone trying to keep me from voting."

You simply nod, then go to your room. You fight back tears as you think about the friends you'll be leaving. And you hope that one day you will all return, when there is less prejudice against Mexican Americans.

94

THE END

To follow another path, turn to page 11.
To read the conclusion, turn to page 103.

"Yes, things are sometimes hard here for us," you say. "But I'd rather try to make things better than leave."

You decide to learn more about what happened in Crystal City in 1963. You also learn about a new group called the Mexican American Legal Defense and Educational Fund (MALDEF). It helps bring lawsuits to protect the rights of Mexican Americans. You read that MALDEF has money to give to Hispanic students who want to study law. That's something you would like to do.

That June you graduate high school. You've made plans to go to a local community college. Then you hope to study at the University of Texas. And in the fall you can vote in local elections for the first time.

Turn the page.

But when you get to the polling place on Election Day, something is wrong. "We don't have your name on the list of registered voters," a woman tells you. "You can't vote."

"But I registered," you say.

"I can only go by what's on the list," the woman says. "They must have made a mistake where you registered."

You feel anger rising inside you. "I bet they didn't make a mistake for the whites who registered."

Another poll worker comes over. "I think you better leave. Or maybe I should call the police?"

➤ To leave, go to page 97.

➤ To stay, turn to page 98.

You feel your face burn with anger as you walk away. But you know it wouldn't be good if the police show up. They might find a reason to arrest you even though you did nothing wrong.

The next day, at the community college, you learn that other students faced the same problem. All of them are Mexican Americans.

"We need to do something about this," your friend Maria says. "We should see if MALDEF will help us."

Some other students nod in agreement. But Robbie says, "Forget using the courts. We should protest, like the blacks in the South did." Robbie looks at you. "What do you think we should do?"

→ To agree with Robbie, turn to page **99**.

→ To agree with Maria, turn to page **100**.

"I am a registered voter," you say. "I have a right to vote. You can't stop me from voting."

"We're just following the rules, chico," the man says.

Chico! That means "boy" in Spanish, but when a Mexican man is called that, it's meant as an insult. "What did you call me?" you say, moving closer.

"I'm calling the police right now!" the woman shouts.

"Do you really want to go to jail for this?" the man asks.

You pull back. Without saying a word, you turn and leave the polling place. Tomorrow you will contact MALDEF and tell them what happened. You want to make sure this never happens again.

THE END

To follow another path, turn to page 11.
To read the conclusion, turn to page 103.

"A protest could be good," you say. "Look at what happened in Crystal City back in '69." The Texas town had again made the news when 2,000 students left their schools to protest discrimination against Mexican Americans. Thanks in part to the protests, the school changed its policies. It hired more Hispanic teachers and let students speak Spanish.

That night you begin to research what other Hispanic groups are doing. You want to play a more active role in making sure Mexican Americans have their right to vote.

THE END

To follow another path, turn to page 11.
To read the conclusion, turn to page 103.

You and Maria go to the MALDEF office in San Antonio. You see white and Hispanic lawyers working together, talking on phones and typing. You approach one of the secretaries and explain why you're there. She doesn't seem surprised that you weren't allowed to vote.

"It happens all the time to Hispanics in Texas," she says. She takes down your name and says that if enough people complain, MALDEF might file a lawsuit. Before you go, you tell her you would like to volunteer at the office. "I want to be a lawyer someday," you say. "This will be good experience."

She smiles and tells you to come back when school is done for the year.

The next summer you stay with friends in San Antonio so you can volunteer at the MALDEF office. You help document cases where Mexican Americans are denied their right to vote.

In 1975 MALDEF officials take that information to Congress. The lawmakers are considering making changes to the 1965 Voting Rights Act. In August Congress votes to extend the law to ensure the voting rights of Spanish speakers as well as blacks. The changes in the law cover Texas and all or part of eight other states.

You feel proud of MALDEF and the work it has done. You begin law school, and you've already begun helping other Mexican Americans defend their rights.

THE END

To follow another path, turn to page 11.
To read the conclusion, turn to page 103.

Many African-Americans registered to vote for the first time in 1965.

CHAPTER 5

THE EFFECTS OF THE VOTING RIGHTS ACT

The Voting Rights Act of 1965 had a huge impact on how many African-Americans registered to vote in the South. In 1965 about 1.9 million blacks were registered to vote. By 1971 the number jumped to almost 3.5 million. By the early 2000s, black voters outnumbered white voters in several southern states. As more blacks voted, more blacks were elected to office.

Hispanic voters increased too. In 1976 the country had just over 2 million Hispanic voters. By 2000 the number was almost 5 million. In part this reflected their growing population. But changes brought by the Voting Rights Act also played a role.

The Voting Rights Act was meant to ensure that all Americans received the right to vote granted in the Constitution. Some states tried to get around parts of the Voting Rights Act, which led to court cases that were finally settled by the U.S. Supreme Court. Overall, the court decisions and later changes to the original Voting Rights Act protected Hispanics and other people who spoke foreign languages, as well as American Indians.

Over time some of the southern states targeted by the law have asked for changes. A section of the Voting Rights Act required the federal government to review new election laws states proposed. In 2013 officials in Alabama won a case in the U.S. Supreme Court that ended the practice of federal review of new election laws. The Supreme Court said it was no longer necessary because the situation had changed in the South. The Voting Rights Act had done its job and blacks no longer faced the discrimination they once did.

But many people disagreed. They noted that the states affected by the Voting Rights Act had tried to pass hundreds of new voting laws that were found to discriminate against some voters. They claimed the 2013 decision came when a number of states were trying to make it harder for black people to vote, not easier.

The Voting Rights Act will remain in place, but more changes to it could come. Even so, it remains one of the most important legal tools ever created in the United States to defend civil rights.

Voters lined up in the 2012 election in which the first black president of the United States, Barack Obama, was re-elected.

Timeline

January 1, 1863—The Emancipation Proclamation is announced by President Abraham Lincoln, releasing all slaves from bondage in the Confederacy. However, with the Civil War still being fought, no slaves are freed at that time.

January 31, 1865—Congress passes the 13th Amendment to the Constitution, abolishing slavery in the United States.

1961—Whites attack civil rights workers trying to end segregation on buses in the South.

1964—January: The 24th Amendment takes effect, ending poll taxes in federal elections.

June: Volunteers to register black voters in Mississippi meet to begin training; three civil rights workers are killed in Mississippi.

July: President Lyndon B. Johnson signs the Civil Rights Act; more than 100 people are arrested during a protest in Greenwood, Mississippi.

August: The Mississippi Freedom Democratic Party tries but fails to take part in the national Democratic Convention.

1965—March 7, "Bloody Sunday": Dozens of civil rights protesters are beaten in Selma, Alabama, as they try to march to the state capitol in Montgomery;

James Reeb of Massachusetts is killed in Selma after he comes to support the Selma marchers; the march is finally allowed to take place, and after, Martin Luther King Jr. speaks to 25,000 people.

June: Volunteers for Summer Community Organizing and Political Education (SCOPE) begin training in Atlanta.

July: Police react violently to civil rights protests in Bogalusa, Louisiana.

August: President Johnson signs the Voting Rights Act.

1968—Mexican Americans who cannot read or write English are not allowed to register to vote in Yakima County, Washington.

1969—Four people who were not allowed to register in Yakima County take county officials to court.

1970—In Garza v. Smith, the U.S. Supreme Court rules that Texas must offer help to voters who can't read the ballot.

1975—Congress changes the Voting Rights Act to offer protection to Hispanics and others who might not speak English well.

2013—The U.S. Supreme Court strikes down part of the 1965 Voting Rights Act, making it easier for some states to pass election laws that could limit voting rights.

OTHER PATHS TO EXPLORE

In this book you've seen how the events surrounding the Voting Rights Act look different from several points of view. Perspectives on history are as varied as the people who lived it. You can explore other paths on your own to learn more about what happened. Seeing history from many points of view is an important part of understanding it.

- Many people who tried to help blacks vote were whites from the North. But some southern whites also opposed discrimination and supported blacks' right to vote. If you were one of those whites, what would you say to friends and family who supported segregation? (Key Ideas and Details)

- The Voting Rights Act of 1965 did not improve voting rights for some American Indians. They started their own civil rights movement. If you were an American Indian, would you take part in this civil rights movement, and why? (Integration of Knowledge and Ideas)

- When the Voting Rights Act was passed, the United States was entering the Vietnam War. Many soldiers were under 21 and too young to vote. Some called for lowering the voting age to 18. Do you think it's fair that someone old enough to fight could not vote? (Integration of Knowledge and Ideas)

READ MORE

Aretha, David. *The Story of the Selma Voting Rights Marches in Photographs.* Berkeley Heights, NJ: Enslow Publishers, 2014.

Hanel, Rachael. *Mexican Immigrants in America: An Interactive History Adventure.* Mankato, Minn.: Capstone Press, 2009.

Hasday, Judy L. *Women in the Civil Rights Movement.* Philadelphia: Mason Crest Publishers, 2013.

Rubin, Susan Goldman. *Freedom Summer: The 1964 Struggle for Civil Rights in Mississippi.* New York: Holiday House, 2014.

INTERNET SITES

Use FactHound to find Internet sites related to this book.
All of the sites on FactHound have been researched by our staff.

Here's all you do:
Visit *www.facthound.com*
Type in this code: 9781491418031

Glossary

ballot (BAL-uht)—paper or mechanical methods used to record a vote

canvass (KAN-vuhss)—to go to many homes seeking support for a cause or to ask residents to do something

civil rights (SI-vil RYTS)—freedoms that all people enjoy in a society

demonstrate (DEM-uhn-strayt)—to join together with others to protest something

discrimination (dis-kri-muh-NAY-shuhn)—the act of treating people unfairly because of their race or gender

harassment (ha-RASS-muhnt)—the act of bothering someone repeatedly

literacy (LIT-ur-uh-see)— the ability to read and write

migrant (MYE-gruhnt)—a person who moves to a new area or country, generally in search of work

picket (PIK-et)—to stand or walk outside a place to protest or demand something

prejudice (PREJ-uh-diss)—an opinion about others that is unfair or not based on facts

racism (RAY-siz-uhm)—the belief that one race is better than another race

segregation (seg-ruh-GAY-shuhn)—the practice of keeping groups of people apart, especially based on race